# THE POWER OF PRAYER

# THE AUTOBIOGRAPHY OF

# ROSLYN STAPLETON

## WITH RUTH TURNER AND ESTHER STAPLETON

To Edith,

This book is for you to come to know the Lord if you don't already know him. I am praying for you. Please read and listen to the CD so that God will make a difference in your life.

God Bless you.

Roslyn Stapleton    30/4/2014

1

Published by James Theophilus Institute

PO Box 9771, Nottingham, NG8 9GY United Kingdom.

Tel: 0115 9783114

ISBN 978-0-9562771-0-7

# Dedication

This book is dedicated to my:

Husband, Bishop James Stapleton

Mother, late Albertha Nembhard

Father, late Charles Vernon

Grand Father, late Enos Vernon

Aunty, Catherine Nembhard

Uncle, late Aston Nembhard

# Contents

## Page One

## Part Two

# Foreword

My Mother, Roslyn Stapleton has been a source of inspiration to our family and friends over many years. Her spiritual guidance is often sought by Christians and those seeking to learn more about Christianity.

Through the years she has shared numerous eventful stories of her witnessing exploits in Nottingham, which have encouraged and strengthened the faith of other Christians who have also embarked on the mission to share the good news of Jesus Christ.

Her ministry of intercession has also touched the lives of countless individuals and they have given reports of how God has transformed their lives and performed miracles.

It is a privilege to have a mother who has demonstrated that living a Christian life can be rewarding and that understanding the scriptures can have a dynamic and profound impact on a person's life.

She has not slowed down in her pursuit of fulfilling the Great Commission and her passion for souls remains her central focus today.

She has shown great commitment and dedication to her Christian faith and I am immensely grateful for her contribution to the Church community. I believe this book will inspire you both spiritually and physically to do the will of God, to stand firm on his word without wavering, knowing that the promises of God are true, and as you allow God to use your gifts, you will see great results.

The bible says that you can do all things through Christ that strengthens you; life can be challenging but the greatest challenge is to answer the call. As you read through this book you will see that dedication and perseverance brings rewards.

**Julianne Stapleton**

# Acknowledgements

This book could not have been written without the support of my daughter's Ruth and Esther.

I would like to thank my husband James and my children, Julianne, Ruth, Jeremy, Peter and Esther for their encouragement.

# *Chapter 1*

## Introduction

My Christian Journey began in St Catherine, Old Harbour Bay, Jamaica where I was born. From an early age I had a close walk with God and he provided a Christian lady that nurtured and developed my understanding of the bible. The late Mrs Lord, a white Christian lady mentored me like the Apostle Paul who instructed Timothy in life skills and ministry. Mrs Lord dedicated her life to the work of the Church and to the community of Old Harbour Bay.

I attended the Baptist Church in Old Harbour Bay with Mrs Lord and participated in church activities, which included teaching a Sunday school class.

There were occasions when I was ridiculed because of the standards I kept, but with God's grace I continued to grow in my faith.

The biblical principles that I learnt were to be the foundation for my future spiritual life in England.

My Mother was very practical and looked for opportunities to develop my skills. She sent me to sewing classes and I became a dressmaker, which was to prove a very useful skill to have both in Jamaica and England. I enjoyed sewing and as I perfected my skills, ladies in Old Harbour would ask me to design dresses for them. Later in life, being able to sew was of great benefit to my family.

## Moving to England

In the early 1960's the British Government invited citizens from the Commonwealth to England, to work and boost the economy. I came to England, leaving behind my family, my mentor Mrs Lord and my friends. It was an exciting time and a great adventure like no other I had ever experienced. In Jamaica I had the opportunity to travel to different parts of country with the church, but this was my first flight on an aeroplane. My mother owned a business in Old Harbour Bay and paid for my flight to travel to England. I arrived at

Heathrow Airport and boarded a train from Kings Cross to Nottingham. I had made arrangements to stay with a friend in Nottingham and arrived late that night. On reaching the house I was knocking and shouting for her to open the door, after a while, a handsome young gentleman came running down the steps, picked up my suitcase and carried it into the house. My friend eventually appeared, we hugged and laughed, she said "you've made it! you've made it!" The young gentleman, who helped me that night, later became my husband.

James originated from the Island of St Christopher, which is also known as St Kitts. He also had a spiritual mentor who nurtured him and gave him spiritual instruction. The late

Pastor William Connor was instrumental in his life, because he lived by example. Pastor Connor had a limited school education; the result of having to leave school to support his family after the death of his father. Problems were further compounded when he lost his left eye working at a soda factory. He had a special love for God and after work; he would help the curate with his duties at St George's Church. When the curate migrated to the Island of St Thomas, William Connor was recruited to fill that position and after serving there for several years he felt the call of God to work amongst the young children in the Island. After reading a book about Robert Raikes, who began the Sunday school movement in Gloucester England in 1735, he was so greatly moved that he decided to start Sunday Schools all around the Island. His towering seven foot frame made him a prominent figure on the Island, he was resourceful and purpose driven and worked to give moral instruction to the young children. He worked in the communities of Basseterre, St Pauls, Lodge Village and Newton Ground helping the poor. He travelled to the United States, Canada and England on several occasions to raise funds for the Sunday Schools by collecting clothes and sponsorship. He was awarded the OBE from the Queen in 1979.

## Working together

Our special love for God was something we had in common from the start of our relationship. We worked hard as a couple dedicating our lives to the service of the Lord, so that his glory could be seen through us. My church background was Baptist and my husband's was Anglican. I heard that there were Pentecostal Churches in Nottingham and decided to visit one to see what it was like. We attended a service at a Pentecostal Church and I enjoyed it so much that I didn't want to return to the Baptist Church. The members of the congregation were operating in the gifts of the spirit, speaking in a heavenly language called 'tongues'. This sparked a longing in my heart for more of God and I began seeking to be filled with the Holy Spirit; by this time we had our first child Julianne.

My husband received a good education at school and this gave him the opportunity to gain employment in an office in Basseterre, St

Kitts, but he was unable to secure this kind of employment in Nottingham.

In order to support the family he took a manual job at the Ministry of Defence in Leicestershire and also attended night school at Peoples College; during this time we made further additions to the family, Ruth, Jeremy and Peter. We worked together to build a strong family unit and a happy home.

## *Chapter 2*

## Answering the call of God

I was longing for a deeper and more meaningful relationship with God, where I could hear his voice. On the 3$^{rd}$ January 1963, whilst I was praying I heard God's voice, He called my name three times, and told me that before he could use me, he would have to put me through a process of purification. I spoke to the minister about the incident and he made reference to 1 Samuel Chapter 3 where God spoke to Samuel and called his name three times, and also gave him prophecies to warn Israel about impending Judgements.

The next development in my spiritual life was different, it was visual; it was a revelation of

God's glory, which was revealed through a cloud that filled the room. It was through this cloud that I saw the face of Jesus. The manifestation of God's glory left an indelible mark on my life and I knew that I wanted more of him.

My focus then turned to getting to know and understand the word of God in more depth. I was drawn to scriptures in the bible that made reference to Jesus fasting and praying. The word of God had a profound affect on my life, I began to fast and pray and I asked God to reveal areas in my life that did not please him. This was the start of the process of purification and once it was completed God started to use me and he gave me spiritual gifts to fulfill the work he assigned.

(1 Corinthians 12v 8-11) The Apostle Paul lists the various gifts of the spirit and these gifts are mentioned throughout the bible. (Romans 12 v 5-8, 1 Corinthians 12 v 8-11, 1 Corinthians 14 v 1-5 Ephesians 4 v 11)

# The Gifts of the Spirit

## Gifts of Revelation

- Faith

- Miracles

- Healing

## Gifts of Power

- The Word of Wisdom

- The Word of Knowledge

- The Discerning of Spirits

## Gifts of Communication

- Prophecy

- Tongues

- Interpretations

## *Chapter 3*

## Speaking in God's heavenly language

### 'Experiencing the power of Pentecost'

For several days I had been praying and fasting for the fulfilment of the Holy Spirit and the gifts of the Spirit; I started to speak in tongues and couldn't stop.  I spoke to the children in tongues and when James came home from work, I spoke to him in tongues. I  experienced the same power of Pentecost that came upon the 120 disciples who began speaking in other languages.

(Acts Chapter 2, 1 v 8)

*'When the Day of Pentecost had fully come, they were all with one accord in one place. And suddenly there came a sound from heaven, as*

*of a rushing mighty wind, and it filled the whole house where they were sitting. Then there appeared to them divided tongues, as of fire, and one sat upon each of them. They were filled with the Holy Spirit and began to speak with other tongues, as the spirit gave them utterance. And there were dwelling in Jerusalem Jews, devout men, from every nation under heaven. And when this sound occurred, the multitude came together, and were confused, because everyone heard them speak in his own language. They were all amazed and marvelled saying to one another. "Look, are not all these who speak Galileans? And how, is it that we hear each in our own language in which we were born?'*

God spoke to me about receiving the gift of Interpretation, (John 14: 16 - 17) in order to translate the words spoken in tongues, into English; the results were miraculous; I began to give interpretations of the tongues and prophecies to the church. The gift of Prophecy is mentioned in (Jeremiah 1 v 11 - 17) (1 Corinthians 14 v 4) this gift refers to the ability to speak a message from God and in some cases to talk about events that have not taken place as yet. One example of this is Isaiah the prophet who prophesied about the birth of Jesus many years before he was born.

God supernaturally gave me additional spiritual gifts. I received dreams and visions and interpreted them to the church as well.

God was speaking through me revealing any sinful activity within the church membership. Those members of the congregation that were not living up to the standards of the bible began to get afraid, and started to spread lies about me, saying that I had been listening to church gossip and  giving false prophecies to the Church. I wasn't interested in listening to gossip, but just said what God wanted me to say, the people who weren't living in line with God's word turned against me. I was listening to the voice of God and not to the people around me.

God spoke to me, to give a message to the minister concerning organising a day of prayer and fasting for the church, before he went away on holiday with his family to Israel. God was directing him to put the church in order before he left. The minister told me that the prophecy wasn't for him and that I should find out who the prophecy was for. The moment the minister left the church building a member of congregation started to confess his sins. The following week I preached about Jonah disobeying God and the congregation started laughing. I found out later that when the minister's daughter went swimming a shark attacked her, bruising her leg. I knew nothing about this incident before preaching at the service, fortunately she was not hurt.

We eventually left that church and started a new church, with a membership that consisted of several families, and we began holding meetings in a shop. We worked together pooling our resources and income together to pay the rent for the shop, although we didn't have a lot of money we sacrificed for the work of God and he supernaturally met our needs.

A funny incident happened at a Sunday service, we were singing a song entitled Fire!! It was about the fire of the Holy Spirit on the day of Pentecost'. A passer by became concerned thinking there was a real fire and called the fire brigade. When the fire men arrived they were surprised to see a small group of people singing a song.

# *Chapter 4*

## Healed from a blood condition

In 1963 I was admitted to the hospital because I was hemorrhaging blood and this could have caused complications for the baby that I was expecting. A team of doctors' carried out various tests, but they couldn't identify the cause of the problem. I was informed by the doctor that my blood group was rare and that they couldn't find a match for my blood type. They put a screen around my bed, but I could still hear the doctors' discussing the prognosis, basically saying that there was no hope of recovery; but I still continued to trust God.

My faith in God was strong and I knew that he would sustain me through this trial. God gave me the patience to endure the test and I never doubted that He would heal me, even though the report wasn't good, I trusted God, because I knew that he never fails.

I put my trust in the creator who created and formed me in his image. Miraculously, God supernaturally healed me and I completely recovered from the blood condition. The nurses on the ward tested my blood on a regular basis and realised that my blood was back to a stable condition. They informed me that a small amount of my blood could save many lives, because it contained a certain antibody that could help people who required blood transfusions. During my stay at the hospital they had taken a lot of blood for testing which I was happy to give, but when I was discharged from the hospital two district nurses' came to see me at home to take more blood for testing. I felt that they had taken enough blood in the past and I prayed to God to give me wisdom to deal with the situation; he gave me the confidence to ask the nurses' who had authorised the blood test, they never returned.

I gave birth to Peter my fourth child a few months later and everything went well. God had completely healed me and I could witness of his enduring love for me. I have all the documentation that illustrates the evidence of my miracle. I am a living example that when the doctors' say No! Jesus says Yes!

The doctors' said that I shouldn't have any more children, but a few years later we had our last child, Esther. We were juggling family work and church life, but God was always faithful. We sacrificed to bring up the children well and encouraged them in their Christian faith and our family prayer meetings, knitted us together.

# *Chapter 5*

## ʻMiracles, signs and wonders'

### The Full Gospel Revival Centre

The membership of the Church increased and we attracted a small number of white people who were living in The Meadows area of Nottingham. They joined the congregation and became very loyal members of the Church. We discovered that there was a Church Hall available to rent in The Meadows area located at 97, Bathley Street. The leaders of the Church agreed to meet Mr Everard who owned the premises to discuss renting the Church Hall, the meeting went well and we were given a date to start renting the Hall for church services. In 1965, we started our new Church and the Church Hall gained the nick name 'The

Tin Church' because of the main structure of the building was made from wood and galvanised steel. The Church grew from a few members into a thriving congregation.

## Miracles, signs and wonders

We experienced many signs and wonders at the Church. Positioned on the platform were four leather chairs for the ministers' and after one Sunday night service, pictures of angels appeared on these chairs, the pictures remained there for three days, it was a glorious time where we experienced the manifestation of God 's glory.

One particular Saturday night, during our testimony service, a lady brought her disabled husband to church and while three teenage girls were singing a song written by Elgar Lewis and William W Rock 'Just lean upon the arms of Jesus He'll help you along' he immediately got out of his wheel chair and began to walk.

I have personally witnessed many miracles in my lifetime, but this specific miracle created a special friendship with Mrs Gennard who lived next door to the church. She had recently lost her husband and God directed me to visit her. When she came to the door she looked very distressed and I felt an overwhelming feeling to comfort her, I said to her that 'Jesus loved her', she expressed with deep sadness, "How can God love me in this situation"? I reached out and hugged her and whispered a prayer. I felt the presence of the Holy Spirit the comforter was there with us, I knew that God was involved in this meeting. Mrs Gennard asked if I would come and see her again. A few days later I went to see her and she said "How did you know that I was hurting?" At that time she was having difficulty sleeping so I encouraged her to read passages from the book of Psalms, she said that she only had a New Testament, I told her that I would pray that God would provide a Bible for her. Miraculously my prayers were answered within a few days, my son Peter came home from college with three Bibles. "Praise the Lord!" another prayer was also answered because there were two children who attended our Sunday school who desperately wanted bibles but couldn't afford them, so God provided for them too.

## Witnessing in the inner city of Nottingham

The witnessing team began with a vision and a mission to share the Good News of the Gospel of Jesus Christ with our friends, neighbours and people in the community. We went into the inner city and surrounding areas to witness (*The term 'to witness' means to share your Christian faith*).

We were bold and courageous and in the face of adversity we put on the armour of God.

We prayed for protection prior to going out into the community to witness. We later learnt how important it was to be covered in prayer. One particular Tuesday evening the team was faced with a violent group of people and a member of the team was punched in the mouth.

God gave me words of knowledge and words of wisdom to answer difficult questions. I was witnessing to a man about the end times, and said "every eye shall behold Jesus" he said "How can we all see Jesus all at the same time?" I told him "We can all see the sun all over the world, that's how we will see Jesus when he returns".

The Apostle Paul makes reference to the gift of the Spirit of Wisdom (1 Corinthians 2 v 6)

This gift is not natural wisdom but super-natural wisdom. This gift can be manifested in several ways Jesus used this gift when the Scribes and Pharisees sought to trip him up with their questions. In the Old Testament King Solomon asked God for the gift of wisdom and Solomon used this gift to identify the real mother of a child.

Jesus through the Holy Spirit gave his disciples Words of Knowledge (1 Corinthians 12 v 8). The Holy Spirit enabled us to operate in this gift when we were faced with difficult questions.

The witnessing team had loyal members who worked together for many years; we would receive requests from friends of the church and other church denominations to visit their homes to hold prayer meetings. At these meetings we would pray for people who wanted to accept Jesus Christ into their lives and for those who wanted to be healed from various sicknesses and diseases. There were occasions when we would be invited to pray for peoples' homes to remove demonic powers and oppression.

(1 Corinthians 12 v 10) (Luke 11) refers to the Gift of Discerning Spirits, this gift which is also evident in the Old Testament to distinguish between true prophets and false prophets.

We were called by God to be prayer warriors and to witness to people who wanted to learn more about Jesus and to operate in the gifts of the spirit.

Over the years we saw the fruit of our labour and many new converts joined the Church and testified of their love for Jesus.

A member of the Church prayed for his wife and children to receive salvation for several years, but it wasn't until after his death that his wife came to know Christ, this happened after several visits to her home by the prayer team.

After going through a period of fasting, praying and intercession, God blessed me with the gift of Healing. (1 Corinthians 12 v 9) He used me to lay hands on people who were sick and dying, who later testified how Jesus Christ had healed them.

The Apostle Paul recorded the exordinary acts of healing in the New Testament. Acts 5v15 gives an account of sick people positioning themselves near Peter to be healed by his shadow when he passed by. God did extraordinary miracles through the Apostle

Paul, his handkerchiefs were given to people and they were healed from diseases.

God used the members of the Church to win their friends and relatives for Christ, many have now died and gone home to be with the Lord, but their legacy still lives on. The seeds that they have sown in the lives of their families and grandchildren have blossomed resulting in many of them becoming ministers of the Gospel.

# *Chapter 6*

## Returning to my homeland of Jamaica

In 1976, I returned to Jamaica, for the first time since leaving my homeland to settle in England. I took my eldest daughter Julianne with me and we visited my family and Mrs Lord.

Mrs Lord lived in a mansion that was set in a beautiful garden. It was just how I remembered it. Mrs Lord came out to greet us; it was wonderful to see her again. She led us into the Great Room for dinner where there were laid out various Jamaican delicacies, cakes and juices. The table was set for a Queen; incidentally James named our daughter after Queen Juliana of the Netherlands. She really did feel like a Queen that day. After the meal Julianne was taken on a tour of the gardens which she enjoyed.

During our holiday, I was invited to preach at the Baptist Church's Women's meeting by Mrs Lord. God blessed the service and three women gave their lives to Jesus.

Mrs Lord was focused on supporting and developing the church, she organised events for the women and young people giving them spiritual instruction. Her enthusiasm for God's work was rewarded with new converts and it was wonderful to hear that her son Peter was now a minister in the USA. God had truly rewarded Mrs Lord in blessing her family.

## *Chapter 7*

## Sharing God's vision for the Church

We pressed forward and we didn't look back as a congregation, we worked hard to refurbish the Church Hall and God blessed the work of our hands. In the late 1970's Mr Everard died and his family put the warehouse next to the Church Hall up for sale. The family tried to sell the warehouse to the City Council, but they were unsuccessful. The Everard Family then approached the church to purchase the warehouse.

God gave me a new vision for the Church which I shared with the leadership, and this was to purchase the warehouse from the Everard Family. However there were members of the congregation who were not optimistic about the prospect of pursuing this new venture. After much prayer and discussion we finally secured a mortgage and brought the warehouse. The next phase of the development plan was to organise the young people into teams, to assist with painting and decorating the inside of the warehouse. Some of the members were not enthusiastic about the way God was leading, but those who were committed to the vision worked hard to clean and clear the building.

The church was growing from strength to strength and new members regularly joined the church. God blessed and prospered the church financially and the leadership was able to purchase new musical equipment, for the music and worship team.

In 1980, an arsonist burnt the Church Hall down and our beloved 'Tin Church' was gone forever. We were insured and we were able to move into the warehouse which became our new home. The news about the fire became known throughout Nottingham and churches rallied around us and supported us with monetary donations, church furniture and chairs.

The Church members operated in the gift of Faith (1 Corinthians 9) in order to move into the next stage of the church development.

The Heroes of faith are listed in (Hebrews 11). This gift was given to men and women in good

measure in the Old Testament. During Jesus'
life on earth there were occasions when he
was amazed by the faith some people had. In
Matthews Gospel Chapter 8 Jesus came in
contact with a centurion whose servant was
sick at home, Jesus offered to go and heal him,
but the Centurion told Jesus to just speak a
word and his servant would be healed
(Matthew 8:10) '....He marvelled and said to
those who followed, assuredly, I say to you, I
have not found such great faith, not even in
Israel'.

# Chapter 8

## My mother receives salvation

In the summer of 1987, we invited my mother Albertha Nembhard to England; she gladly accepted the invitation to spend time with us, meeting James and her Grandchildren for the first time. Since this was her first holiday abroad, I arranged for my Uncle Aston Nembhard to travel with her. It was a great experience for my mother to visit England, to see the sights and also attend church. She was aware that Jesus loved her, but she had not taken the steps to accept Him into her life as her personal saviour. For many years I prayed for her and was encouraged by the scripture that says that "*And whatever things you ask in prayer, believing, you will receive."* **(Matthew 21 v 22)**

My mother had the opportunity to see the family taking part in church programmes, singing worship songs, testifying about the goodness of God and preaching about his faithfulness. I was overwhelmed with happiness that my mother was able to experience these services as well as listen to the testimonies of the members of the congregation.

On her final visit to our church, she was invited to the front of the church by the ministry team to receive a prayer of protection for her flight back home to Jamaica. When we returned to our seats a member of the congregation came to me and whispered that God had just given her a vision that my Mother was destined for eternal life. This was a confirmation that my prayers had been answered and that my mother would receive salvation.

When my mother returned to Jamaica, she accepted the Lord Jesus Christ into her life and in 1988, she was baptised at the Zion Revival Church in Old Harbour Bay, St Catherine, Jamaica, It was a joy and delight for me and my family.

In 1989, she died and went to be with the Lord. When I attended my Mother's funeral hundreds of people were there, and many testified about her conversion and how she faithfully served God until the end of her life. I mourned her passing, but I was comforted to know that God had indeed heard my prayers.

# Chapter 9

## Intercultural Theology Course

## CONTRAST

I returned to learning in my late 50's, it was my prayer partner who recommended that we studied the CONTRAST course together. (CONTRAST - Christians of Nottingham Training and Studying Together). We researched theological information for the bible course and with the support of our daughters typing our assignments we completed our course work.

God blessed us with confidence and to our amazement the lecturers expressed how surprised they were at the depth of knowledge and understanding we had of the scriptures. We were encouraged to participate in class discussions and we were able to give our views and opinions on various topics.

We learnt about Judaism and Catholicism and had an opportunity to go on trips to the Holocaust Centre in Newark, Nottinghamshire and to St Bernard's Monastery in Leicestershire.

As the course progressed I started to gain a better understanding of the origins of the Baptist Church in Jamaica. Through my research of the Baptist Church I discovered that George Liele an African American slave who arrived in Jamaica in 1783 founded the Baptist Church. He started his pioneering work in Kingston. George Liele's work of evangelism was expanded when he appointed three workers to assist him, Moses Baker, Thomas Swigle and George Gibbs. Their earliest efforts were concentrated around the eastern parts of Jamaica. It was interesting to find out that they went to Parish of St Catherine where I was born. Their work was not always welcomed by the planters but many slaves were converted. I have discovered from further research the significance of George Liele's contribution to the religious history of Jamaica. The work of George Liele later received support from Baptist movement overseas which helped to establish the Jamaican Baptist Mission in 1814. Learning about Caribbean Church history developed my understanding of how different churches came to be established in Jamaica.

This course enabled me and my prayer partner to learn more about other Christian traditions, we worked hard and obtained good grades for our assignments.  We both graduated from the two year course receiving a Certificate in Intercultural Studies from the University of Nottingham. I was asked by a lecturer at the graduation  what I was going to do next, I have always had the desire to write a book, well it has taken a little longer than I expected but this is God's season.

This book, I hope will encourage older people to return to learning because we have a wealth of knowledge and life experience to impart to the community and the church.

This is a short extract from an assignment submitted for the Certificate of Intercultural Theology (CONTRAST Course) *Question: 'Describe examples of missionary activity from your own tradition. Comment on how the community of a shared life in Christ is built up through service, dialogue and liberation'*

In order to describe the above it is important to gain an understanding of what a missionary activity is. The word MISSION means sending. God sends missionaries worldwide to proclaim the good news, to offer God's love through service, dialogue and liberation, and to build up a community of shared life in Christ. In the Gospel of Matthew it describes the great commission. Matthew 28 v 16, '....He told his disciples, I have been given all authority in heaven and in earth. Therefore go and make disciples in all nations, baptising them in the name of the Father and the Son and of the Holy Spirit, then teach these disciples to obey all commands I have given you; and be sure of this that I am with you always, even to the end of the world' Therefore Jesus gave his disciples instructions concerning the propagation of the gospel, He informed them, that they had a duty to tell others about the Gospel and teach them in order that they could teach others. The Baptist Church embraced everyone irrespective of their colour or background, many Baptists made it their mission to take the Gospel to different parts of the world. In 1782 George Liele a former slave came and initiated the Baptist Church in Jamaica preaching to the slaves. [1] William Carey (1761 – 1834), an English Baptist, devoted most of his life to

---

[1] Perspectives on the world of Christian Movement Chapter 43 page 288 by David Cornelius

taking the gospel to India. He involved the native preachers in spreading the gospel. He told people to "Expect great things from God; attempt great things for God". [2] I converted to Pentecostalism when I arrived in England and my experience of mission activity within this tradition emphasised the importance of the Holy Spirit. Act 1 v 8 Jesus told his disciples 'When the Holy Spirit comes upon you ,you will receive power to testify about me with great effect, to the people in Jerusalem, through out Judea, about my death and resurrection.' The

---

[2] Perspectives on the world of Christian Movement page 288 Chapter 44 page 293 Edited by Ralph D Winter & Steven C Hawthorne.

Holy Spirit gives us guidance on how to converse with people.

In 1906, Joseph Seymour was the minister of a small fellowship and the Holy Spirit fell like a blot of lightening and the members began to speak in tongues and prophesying, this out pouring started one of the greatest revivals known in history (1906 – 1909 Azusa Street Revival, Los Angeles). The Pentecostal movement is also based firmly on missionary work. In many countries around the world Pentecostal missionaries proclaim the good news of Jesus Christ. Albert Benjamin Simpson (1843 – 1919) founded the Christian and Missionary Alliance. He was well known for his various publications and views on the gifts of the Holy Spirit. He urged believers to pray for a special manifestation of the Holy Spirit. [3]

*In 1998, I received a certificate in Intercultural studies from the University of Nottingham.*

---

[3] A B Simpson And The Pentecostal Movement – Charles W. Nienkirchen 1992 Page 65)

# *Chapter 10*

## My miraculous recovery from a stroke

In 2003, we were preparing to travel to Jamaica it was an extremely busy period, especially getting organised for the trip.

I was in my bedroom and suddenly everything went dark and I felt myself falling. I heard the doorbell and somehow I got myself to the stairs, and down the steps. My son Jeremy was at the door, I managed to open it and he supported me whilst we waited for the ambulance. My daughter Ruth arrived a few moments later and prayed for me. At the hospital, they conducted numerous tests and said I had a mini stroke, but was well enough to be discharged. God was looking after me and I felt strong enough to carry on as normal and went out to the shops the next day. My family supported me with their prayers and I received many miracles making it possible for us to maintain our travel plans to Jamaica.

On arrival at the airport James sorted out the passports and travel documents, whilst my daughter Esther made enquiries about special travel arrangements for us.

We stayed with my Aunty Catherine and had a wonderful time, travelling to various parishes in Jamaica.

God is my healer and I am back to full strength, doing the Lord's work like Caleb, we are never too old to do the work of God. '*All that God requires of us is obedience and faith to please*

**him.'** **Joshua Chapter 14: 6-12 gives an account of the great man of faith.**

At the age of 85, Caleb took possession of a section of land after winning a battle to obtain it. Caleb is known for his courage and faith in the bible, because he was one of the spies that gave Moses a good report about possessing the land of Canaan.

My favourite hymn is *'I believe the true report'* **by C.P Jones (Redemption Hymnal)** there are numerous songs of faith that have kept me going through the trials of life. I serve a faithful saviour who has been good to me. We serve a God who performs supernatural miracles. Praise him for the miracles he is bringing your way.

# *Chapter 11*

## Promotion comes from God
## Lord Mayor's Chaplain
## Bishop James Stapleton

In Jamaica, I prayed for a husband that would serve God and he granted my request. James has been working tirelessly and diligently in partnership with different churches for many years. His interest in the wider church community started in St Kitts as a member of the St George Anglican Church. He enjoyed learning about different denominations on the Island by visiting the Baptist, Methodist, Moravian, Catholic and Wesleyan churches. To develop his knowledge of scriptures he studied biblical studies before moving to England.

Whilst James dedicated his life to ecumenical service; I gave my life to the ministry of intercessory prayer, praying for him and supporting him in his work **'For _with God nothing is impossible.' (Luke 1v 37)_**

God granted James favour with the leaders of other major churches and they have invited him to join their committees, to preach and give lectures at their churches.

Tuesday 11th July 2000, we were invited to attend a service of celebration and thanksgiving in honour of the 100th Birthday of the late Queen Mother, Her Majesty Queen Elizabeth I at St Pauls Cathedral London. It was a wonderful experience of which we have fond memories.

In 2002, James was instrumental in organising a service at the Mansfield Road Baptist Church to celebrate Her Majesty Queen Elizabeth II Golden Jubilee and Jamaica's 40th Anniversary of Independence.

James was consecrated to the office to Bishop in 2002 for his ecumenical work, community action, civic services and spiritual support to businesses. Within the same year he launched a new ministry, The Open Christian Fellowship based in Nottingham with a mission to work closely with community organisations and churches in the region.

He received a special appointment to become Chaplain to the Lord Mayor of Nottingham Councillor Des Wilson on two occasions 2002 - 2003 and 2006 -2007.

In 2007, James worked with the Parish Church of St Mary The Virgin in Nottingham to organise an event to mark the bicentenary of the abolition of the slave trade. In attendance was The Bishop of Kingston, Jamaica, The Rt Revd Robert Thompson, representatives from the civic, political life, church leaders and community organisations. The service concluded with the re-dedication of the grave of George Africanus, a slave born in Sierra Leone who later became an entrepreneur in Nottingham. James was also invited to join a committee at the Nottingham City Council to organise additional events to mark the abolition of the slave trade.

# *Chapter 12*

## Photographs

Late Mrs Lord and Mr Lord outside the Baptist
Church, Old Harbour, Jamaica 1975

Revd James Stapleton &      72      Revd William Conner Preaching
Revd William Conner 1979            at Full Gospel Revival Centre
                                    1979

James, Ruth, my mother Albertha, Julianne, Esther, Roslyn, Peter, Natasha 1987

Jeremy and my mother Albertha Nembhard 1987

Bishop James Stapleton, Lord Mayor of Nottingham
Councillor Des Wilson and Lady Mayoress Ms Cecile
Henry Bourne 2006

Roslyn Stapleton and Bishop James Stapleton
St Mary's Church 2006

Bishop James Stapleton & Rt Rev Robert Thompson Bishop of Kingston Jamaica 200th Anniversary of the abolition of the slave trade St Mary's Church 2007

The re-dedication of the grave of George Africanus High Commissioner Whiteman, Lady Mayoress Ms Henry Bourne & Lord Mayor Des Wilson 2007

# Part Two

# Chapter 1

## How to become a Christian

If you would like to know how to become a Christian and live a Christian life read Romans 10: 9-10 which states:

*'That if you confess with your mouth the Lord Jesus and believe in your heart that God has raised Him from the dead, you will be saved.*

*For with the heart one believes unto righteousness, and with the mouth confession is made unto salvation.'*

**Therefore to become a Christian you must:**

- Believe that Jesus is the son of God

- Believe that he rose from the dead

- Repent and turn from your sins

   (Tell him you are sorry for things you have done wrong)

- Follow him – The stories of his life and teachings give examples for you to follow.

(Acts 16 v 27 – 34)

The Apostle Paul said to the Philippian Jailor who wanted to know to how to be saved, "Believe in the Lord Jesus Christ and you will be saved." The word "believe" means not only give mental assent to Jesus Christ as Lord and Saviour of your life, but it means to live by his teachings. We can only do this when we are transformed, or as the bible states "saved". We cannot do this by ourselves we need Jesus to live in us. We take him by faith, but faith finds expression in "good works". Jesus said let your light so shine before men that they may see your good works and glorify your father which is in heaven." When he comes to live in us, his goodness and his righteousness starts to operate within us.

By saying this prayer you can ask Jesus to come into your life.

'Dear Lord Jesus I recognise that I am a sinner and I am sorry for the sins that I have committed. I am willing to turn from everything that I know is wrong. Thank you for dying on the cross for me and I ask you to come into my life. Forgive me, cleanse me and strengthen me, and from this moment I accept you as Lord and Saviour. Amen.'

There are three things that will help you grow as a Christian

- Reading the Bible

- Talking to God in Prayer

- Meeting with other Christians

# Chapter 2

## Experience the power of

## God for yourself

**How to pray**

To pray is simply talking with God. The bible teaches us how to pray. There are many prayers in the bible the most famous prayer is the **Lords Prayer**. Jesus knew how important prayer was, he prayed to God the father on many occasions in the New Testament. Jesus prays for us, and intercedes for us to the Father on our behalf.

# The Lord's Prayer

*Our Father which art in heaven, hallowed be thy name. Thy kingdom come. Thy will be done in earth as it is in heaven. Give us this day our daily bread. And forgive us our trespasses as we forgive those who trespass against us. And lead us not into temptation, but deliver us from evil: For thine is the Kingdom, and the power, and the glory, for ever. Amen.*

Matthew Chapter 6 verses 9 – 13 (NKJV)

## Why is praying so important

Prayer is very important because through prayer we are fighting battles in the invisible realm that is why the devil does not want us to pray.

## Revivals in England

John and Charles Wesley, along with George Whitefield, began historic prayer meetings, and a mighty revival resulted in England. Prayer can alter the course of history.

The bible is filled with examples of nations changed through the power of prayer. When Daniel arrived on the scene in Babylon, little did he realise the future impact of his prayers. Daniels prayers opened the path for restoration of Israel.

## How to become a Prayer Warrior

Becoming a prayer warrior takes discipline, but it is essential to our spiritual development. It can be a personal activity which requires allocating a specific time of the day for intercession which may include worshipping and giving thanks to God. Spending time with God reaps spiritual benefits and helps us overcome spiritual battles.

## The Holy Spirit

The Holy Spirit is present on earth he is the comforter, the teacher that helps us in our walk with God. The Holy Spirit works on our behalf when we pray and he fights for us in the invisible realm.

## What are spiritual battles?

Spiritual battles are forces of evil that are around us, their main aim is to stop and hinder us from having a deeper relationship with God. When we pray to God He fights our spiritual battles.

# Chapter 3

## Faith Enrichment

## Sermons by Ruth Turner

### Be Focused

Ask God for wisdom and a vision for the future. Let God influence your decision, even if it means taking a risk. God will bless the seed, the individual that sows the seed, and the reaper.

### Staying afloat

Loving God gives us a passion to love the life that God has blessed us with. The Bible makes reference to this, as a believer we can live a life of safety. The Psalmist David says.

*'The name of the Lord is a strong tower and when the righteous runs into it they are safe'*

In the sixteenth chapter of Genesis it states that Noah was a just man and prefect in his generations, and the earth was filled with violence. In verse fourteen God said to Noah.

"Make thee an ark of gopher wood, rooms shalt thou make in the ark, and shalt pitch it within and without with pitch."

God gave Noah a divine plan of safety and escape for his family and a new generation of creatures during the flood which began in his 600th year and lasted for 40 days and 40 nights. After which the ark came to rest on a mountain range known as Ararat (Armenia)

Noah later built an altar unto the Lord and sacrificed burnt offerings God promised never to destroy mankind again by flood. Keeping true to your calling will enable you to stay in the plan of God and he will ensure that you stay afloat.

## The Call

A call is hearing the voice of God in your spirit which gives spiritual guidance and instruction, responding to this call will give positive and productive results. There are several ways to seek out the call of God for your life.

1.  Seek the Lord in prayer, fasting, reading and studying of the word of God.

2.  When God feels that you are spiritually mature, he begins the process to separate you for a specific ministry by providing a spiritual coach to support you.

3      Your call may be divinely orchestrated has in the case of young Samuel in the temple or Saul the persecutor of the believers on the Damascus road.

Isaiah Chapter 43 v 1

"But now thus saith the Lord that created thee Oh Jacob, and he that formed thee O Israel fear not: for I have redeemed thee. I have called thee by thy name; thou art mine."

This scripture puts the call of God on our life into perspective; when you are aware how special you are to God and the Kingdom. He his looking for raw talent to use, he needs your commitment to shape your life, a day at a time, so his glory can shine through you.

## Called to be God's mouthpiece

God is looking for individuals that are ordinary when compared to their peers (some would say average), but extra-ordinary in the eyes of God.

God calls individuals that feel insignificant in their own eyes, and are on the run from their call to be his mouthpiece.

Many were tried, proven and tested like Abraham, Jacob and Joseph and endured the pressure of the call of God. In the 12$^{th}$ Chapter of Hebrews they are called the **hero's of faith.**

God provided a window of opportunity for Isaiah to recognise his new commission; in sixth Chapter of Isaiah it gives reference to this.

'In the year King Uzziah died, Isaiah saw the Lord in a vision in all his glory. And the heavenly host in worship to the Lord crying Holy is the Lord.

Isaiah cried out woe is me, I am ruined, after the purging process, he was ready for the call to be God's mouthpiece. God was now woven into the tapestry of Isaiah's life.'

## The mind of Christ

Having the mind of Christ is having the ability to think, how Christ wants you to think.

Commitment to Christ and his desire for our life is through total surrender to him, and adopting the mind of Christ and applying Christ to our everyday thought process.

I Corinthians Chapter 2 verse 16

"For who has known the mind of the Lord that he may instruct him but we have the mind of Christ. It is a total mystery to man how the mind of Lord works, but we can be sure that he will work in the interest of the believers. Having our mind set on worldly ambitions will drive us further away from having the mind of God; it might take a while before we recognise that having a mind focused on God brings fruitful results.

## The Anointing

Some believers describe the anointing as a mantle blessing or a double portion that Elisha received after he saw Elijah being taken up in a chariot of fire into heaven.

**In the action Gospel "Acts"** the disciples of Jesus waited eagerly in anticipation for the promise from the Father the "Comforter".

"But ye shall receive power after that the Holy Ghost is come upon you".

On the day of Pentecost the wind of the Holy Spirit filled the upper room and the divine fire fell on them, filling them up with the Holy Spirit.

The manifestation resulted in them speaking in a new heavenly language.

They were then sent out as ambassadors to the nations of the world to evangelise, speaking with confidence and boldness and a new wave of revival started among the Jews and the Gentiles.

Once a believer has received the anointing, one has to seek for a refilling of the anointing, so that the administration of the gifts is kept alive, for the deliverance of individuals in Jesus.

The authority comes from the

1.    The Son of God

2.    The Son of Man

3.    The Divine Teacher

4.  The Great Physician

5.  The Bread of Life

6.  The Water of Life

7.  The Light of the World

8.  The Good Shepherd

God wants his believers to occupy until he comes, he his sending anointed men and women to the community in which they live to bring people who desire to be a friend of God.

## Do you have the Staying Power?

Many of today's leaders would refer to staying power as perseverance and stamina, working hard without receiving any form of recognition.

Composer George Frederic Handel was bankrupt when in 1741 a group of Dublin Charities offered him commission to write a musical piece for a benefit performance to raise funds to free men from a debtor's prison. He accepted that commission and gave himself tirelessly to work on it. In just 24 days, Handel composed the well-known masterpiece "Messiah" which contains "The Hallelujah Chorus" a scripture from the Wisdom Book of Job "I know that my Redeemer lives – and that in the end he will stand upon the earth".

God has equipped us with endurance, when you feel at your lowest and you want to give up that is when he is busy working things out for you.

Offer up praise and thanksgiving to the Lord until you feel that your victory is nigh at hand.

## Untouchable

Without the sense of touch our sense of danger is no longer heightened. The human body works in unison enabling all the senses to complement each other.

Without the sense of feeling one of the other senses as to rise to bridge the gap for example the sense of sight is heightened to see danger and sends signals to the brain to warn of impeding disaster.

God makes provision for us; he touches us and injects joy and happiness into our life.

Psalms 105 v 15 speaks about his protection for his anointed children "Saying touch not mine anointed and do my prophets no harm"

If an individual dares to touch one of God's anointed they have God to answer to. God says you can look, but you cannot touch, the ring of anointing around you will make you untouchable.

Once God has stepped into the life of his chosen possession he has warned the devil, don't mess or I will deal with you. God can touch, but he does not want any one to touch.

God can temporally move the hedge, to prove, your faithfulness to him, and put back the hedge, to releases an anointing, you have never experienced before for his glory alone.

## Jesus is the answer

"For every question there is an answer"

We have questions – but the likelihood is that we will already know the answer.

 "To every problem there is a solution"

God corresponds with us on a daily basis, through our thoughts, actions and divine interventions.

St John Chapter 14 v 5

"Thomas said to him Lord we don't know where you are going so how can we know the way" Jesus said in his words " I am the way the truth and the life no one comes to the father except through me"

We have a friend in Jesus that is the answer to our problems. Jesus is committed to respond, not in a way that we may want, but answer he will.

## Trust in the Lord

To put your trust in someone is to have reliance in the integrity of that person. To trust in the Lord calls for discipline, and an individual that trusts God and agrees with others in prayer encourages God to intervene.

Psalms Chapter 12 v 7 says

"Some trust in chariots and some in horses, but we will trust in the name of the Lord God".

Having a false trust causes limitations in the life of the believer – material things serve a purpose, but they are perishable, it is vital that nothing takes God's place in our lives.

Trust is an active word, engaging in prayer and intercession to the Lord and waiting patiently for a response that will bring maximum results in a believer's life.

# True Worshipper

Every individual is born with an innate sense to worship. Without a specific knowledge of Jesus Christ their energy and drive is otherwise directed to other religions, or material things, houses and land. They become fans of Pop Stars and Celebrities and they begin to worship them.

The Psalmist David loved to worship and every beat of his heart was in melody with his praise to God.

Psalms 96 v 6 - brings worship to God to the fore.

"O come, let us worship and bow down, let us kneel before the Lord our maker".

In this Psalm David invites us as God's people to worship and Praise God and to offer thanksgiving to him with respect and humility.

True worshippers will acknowledge their short comings and are aware that God will step in when they take time out to praise him.

## Taking up the Challenge

The word challenge means to take the initiative to compete and to rise up in the middle of opposition and trial to be a conqueror.

God develops us and prepares us for the task ahead. He gives us the grace to endure and the faith and fortitude to continue.

The Holy Spirit equips us with the gifts of wisdom, knowledge and understanding and heightens the gift of discerning within us.

The Latin word for courage is **"Cor"** which means heart. Take heart you are not alone when facing adversity and challenges. When Joshua succeeded Moses has the leader of the Children of Israel the Lord reassured Joshua with these words "Be strong and courageous I will support you in leading these people" Take courage in the confidence that God alone is your strength.

It is always going to be a challenge to lead people that do not want to be led and a large percentage of their life is spent in the wilderness of moaning and complaining.

## The Power of the Blood of Jesus

It is a known fact that life is in the blood. Without the blood flowing through your veins life ebbs away. To have Power means to have strength, energy and vigour.

Matthew Chapter 26 v 28

God prepares the Church for a greater destiny in gaining power through the precious blood of Jesus Christ.

"This is my blood of the covenant, which is poured out for many for the forgiveness of sin".

Human forgiveness means the remission of a penalty deserved, whereas the divine forgiveness in type and fulfilment in both Old and New Testament always follows the execution of the penalty. The priest will make an atonement for him for the sin he has committed and he will be forgiven.

This is the blood of the covenant, which is poured out for many for the forgiveness of sin. The sin of the justified believer interrupts his fellowship it is forgiven upon confession, but always on the ground of Christ's propitiatory sacrifice.

# Spirit of Discernment

\*     The Spirit is the mind of the soul

\*     Discernment is spiritual perception

Our five senses help's us to discern and empower us to live in the environment we live in.

- Sense of Touch

- Sense of Smell

- Sense of Taste

- Sense of Hearing

- Sense of Sight

The Holy Spirit equips us for our spiritual journey with Christ on this earth. He heightens our spiritual senses, so we are aware of what to touch.

Our growth in God and the word of God brings revelation of his Son Jesus Christ to the fore and aid our spiritual development to see natural and spiritual forces working against us and others.

1 Corinthians Chapter 12 verse 10

To another working of miracles, to another prophesy to another discerning of spirits, to another diver's kinds of tongues to another the interpretation of tongues.

# True Prosperity

- True means genuine.
- Prosperity means successful and rich.

Putting Jesus Christ in first place in our lives produces true prosperity.

- Believing by faith through Jesus Christ develops us.
- The Holy Spirit builds our character.
- God brings richness through his word.
- Purging of our roots produces fruit in abundance.
- Tested to the point of breaking we are proved to see whether we are worthy of our calling.

## God is not limited

To put a limit on God is like trying to grasp the rays of the sun in one hand. 'How can finite man limit an infinite God?'

God is only limited to our imagination but when we understand how powerful he truly is then our imagination is freed so that we are enabled to accomplish great things by his power.

God gave us some information in the Bible about himself, he said that 'no man can see me and live.' This suggests that an encounter with him is very dangerous for us. Moses in spite of this asked to see God, so God hid him in the mountain and walked by him, so Moses saw God's back. The results were amazing. The Bible tells us that Moses face shone so much after this encounter that he put a cloth on his face.

What is exciting is that Jesus Christ lived among us for 33 years. When he left this earth he gave his people power to speak his word with authority, power over sickness and victory over sin. We all need to recognise that this power does not have its root in us but in the all powerful God and this is the reason we are thankful.

God is the Alpha and Omega which is translated the beginning and the ending. Genesis begins with the progressive self revelation of God and Christ Elohim, Jehovah and Adonai

In Genesis 1 v 1

"In the beginning God created the heavens and the earth"

He also created man 'Adam' the beginning of life. God had the whole provision of nature, animals and human life in mind.

He did not restrict their growth; he took pleasure in their development until the serpent tempted Eve to eat of the tree of knowledge of good and evil. Adam and Eve now had to work for their bread which was still in abundance. God did not limit their resources and continued to bless their harvest.

We have experienced the magnitude of God's greatness and he is still the God of more than enough.

## Peace be unto you

It is the blessing of God bestowed upon believers who are the friends of Christ. Peace with God personifies everything about the blessed and quiet assurance of God in the present and the future of our life.

The peace of God is within us, it is like still water that runs deep into the body, soul and spirit. We have to cultivate a passion and drive for the peace of God through prayer, intercession and meditation on the Word of God.

The Peace of God that passes all understanding will keep our heart and mind pure in the knowledge of our Lord Jesus that is the Head of the Church.

## The best is yet to come

How do we define the best one, we can describe it has excellent.

On our pursuit for happiness we can be excited in the knowledge

*       Victories out weigh our set backs.

*       Triumphs out weigh our challenges.

*       Blessing out weigh our disappointments.

*       The future is bright for every believer. (Rainbow bright)

*       The best is yet to be revealed in us.

*       Never give up ride the storm with dignity.

*       The best in us will influence our dreams and desires.

*    It will give us fresh insight and a fresh
     perspective.

*    The Holy Spirit will cause a fresh fire to
     come to the fore.

*    The choices we make will define us for
     eternity.

## Representing the Kingdom

We represent the kingdom with a true conviction, surrendering to the call of God upon our life.

- We are more than a Delegate

- We are more than a Congressman

- We are more than a Diplomat

We are citizens of Heaven 24 hours a day, 7 days a week we are giving true homage to the Servant King while on our spiritual pilgrimage.

In the Gospel of Luke 19 verse 13 in the parable of the pound. The Nobleman gave his ten servants an opportunity to serve by giving them 10 pounds and said unto them "Occupy until I come"(inhabit, keep busy, take up an occupation) "Be not weary in well doing for you shall reap if you faint not".

Everyday God is sending us to the nations in word & deed. God is calling us to be his ambassadors, the parable highlighted the servants who had neglected their duty to serve and had missed an opportunity to represent the kingdom.

Your life represents the beauty of Jesus and as a result people are drawn to the kingdom. The negative message about Christ by the humanist has started the big search to know the truth. People are watching the representatives of the kingdom and following the light to Jesus Christ.

## God's Power in Warfare

Power means to have influence and authority. In the time of complacency or in peace time, people forget about God and begin to invest their energy and time in new exploits.

God whips up a storm. In the Bible we have illustrations when the Israelites turned away from Yahweh and they began to worship idols. Their enemies whose armies who were much bigger and more powerful than them started to make threats of war against Israel this is when the Israelites began to pursue God for help.

In the book of Chronicles in the Old Testament the Kings had significant roles to play in protecting their cities from hostile nations, and also capturing other nations. Jehoshaphat had great wealth and honour but he was only ailed to Ahab by marriage. King Ahab asked Jehoshaphat to support him in capturing Ramoth Gilead. Jehoshaphat responded to his request, but he wanted to first seek the counsel of the Lord.

They sought the counsel of the Lord through Micaiah, but the word of the Lord prophesied was not tempered for their taste. Ahab did not like the truth and was more interested in the lying spirit that came from his counsellors. Ahab told Jehoshaphat to wear his garments, because of mistaken identity Jehoshaphat nearly lost his life. Ahab was defeated and he died at Ramoth Gilead.

When God speaks he means what he says. God is a man of his word it is a shame that Ahab did not recognise this before his premature death.

## The Messiah

Isaiah made mention of the coming Messiah in the 9$^{th}$ chapter of his writings.

"For unto us a child is born, unto us a son is given and the government shall be upon his shoulder, and his name shall be called Wonderful, Counsellor, The Mighty God, The Everlasting Father, and the Prince of Peace."

"Of the increase of his Government and peace there shall be no end, upon the throne of David, and upon his kingdom, to order it and to establish it with judgement and with justice from henceforth even forever. The zeal of the Lord of hosts will perform this"

400 years had passed since Isaiah prophesied about the coming Messiah. Isaiah refers to the Messiah (Jesus Christ) as the great light. In the time of darkness God promised to send light to shine on all people living in the shadow of death. This message of hope was fulfilled in the birth of Christ and the establishment of his eternal kingdom.

In our time of personal darkness, life challenges, pain, sickness and distress Jesus is our light that shines on our situation .Isaiah uses five names to describe the Messiah.

| | |
|---|---|
| **Wonderful** | He is exceptional, distinguished without an equal. |
| **Counsellor** | He is an Adviser to all who accepts his advice |
| **The Mighty God** | He is God himself |
| **The Everlasting Father** | He is timeless, he is God our Father |
| **The Prince of Peace** | His Government is one of Justice and Peace |

The birth of Jesus Christ in Bethlehem was the fulfilment of prophecies in the Gospels.

God gave his only son as a gift and present to the world it was a time of celebration of praise and worship.

In Luke's Gospel the angel of the Lord announced the arrival of the Saviour which is Christ the Lord to the shepherds, the angels and the heavenly hosts were having a concert of praise and worship to God.

The wise men in Matthew's Gospel followed the star from the East signifying the birth of Jesus. The gifts that they brought symbolized Christ's identity and what he would accomplish.

- Gold was a gift for a King
- Frankincense a gift for Deity
- Myrrh a gift for a man that was going to die.

The wise men worshipped Jesus for who he was. Jesus was a gift to the world. Ask yourself – 'Are you presenting yourself as a gift to Jesus today?'

## God's Way

It takes a Godly person to follow God's way, God's principles, God's purpose, God's wisdom and God's plan. Man's ways can never be compared to the direction of God.

Solomon was a wise man. When he commenced his journey to become the King of Israel he asked for wisdom. He received from God both wisdom and wealth, but his wives led him away from God's way.

"The steps of a good man is ordered by the Lord"

Turn back and follow God's way, know who you believe in and be persuaded that he can do all things well. Temptation and trouble can temporarily cause us to lose focus.

Trusting God and praying and reading the Living Word gives us focus and a fresh perspective.

In the Wisdom Proverb chapter 3 v 6 states "In all your ways acknowledge him and he will make your path straight".

This is the reward of wisdom, God's way.

## Standing Still

"Be still and know that I am God"

Standing still takes practice. Impatience is a major factor in hindering one from standing still.

Standing still bears significant results it builds:-

- Confidence

- Stature

- Stamina

- Perseverance

Standing still helps us to focus on what God wants for us. It helps us to recognise how insignificant we are and it is the Almighty God that has the ability to change situations.

"Stand still and see the Salvation of the Lord".

Psalm 46 v 10 says

"God is our refuge and strength a very present help in trouble".

Standing still and seeing the Salvation of the Lord is another word for waiting on the Lord.

"Wait on the Lord and be of good courage and he shall strength thy heart"

We are encouraged to stand still and be strong.

## In Due Season

The Key to every season of life is preparation. There are 4 seasons to the year

- Spring

- Summer

- Autumn

- Winter

We buy seeds and plant it in the soil, we tend to them with tender love and care, watering, giving nutrients when required. We admire the growth and wait in anticipation for the flowers or fruit to appear, and then we give God thanks for the harvest.

In Apostle Paul's writing to the Galatian Christians he tells them in chapter 6 v 9 "And let us not be weary in well doing for in due season we shall reap if we faint not".

In the right season when your fruit is ripe, you will receive your reward, your blessing and your spiritual inheritance. Working hard can either be a pleasant experience or a painful experience, but determination with God's help is the key to your success.

When faith is birthed, opportunity will arise to meet you. Investment and grace will be harvested through you. When due season is revealed within you, running away is always an easy option.

God is always thinking good thoughts towards you; with Jesus your future is secure.

## A Promise

- Promise and Possession

- Promise and Promotion

In Hebrews 10 v 23 states

"Let us hold unswervingly to the hope we profess, for he who promised is faithful"

A promise from the Almighty without compromise, because he has made a pledge with you, he will not neglect his vow. God will never overlook the beauty of the future of your reward. Your destiny is important to him.

Hebrews Chapter 11 v 11

"By faith Abraham, even though he was past age, and Sarah herself was barren, was enabled to become a father because he considered him faithful who had made the promise".

## Faith X Promise = Completion

God told Abraham to go to a place he would later receive as his inheritance. Abraham had to go through a progression of his faith.

You may be familiar with the saying 'Points means Prizes', but it takes obedience to the word of the Lord for your faith in God to mature and pursue his best.

## Our Spiritual Inheritance

Without Salvation there is no guarantee of receiving a spiritual inheritance. We are joint heirs and our spiritual legacy comes from our Heavenly Father. Every test that God has helped us to win and every trial he has shielded us from, brings us closer to our spiritual heritage.

You can either be spiritual rich or spiritual poor, but you will be rewarded for fighting the good fight of faith.

Genesis Chapter 15 verse 1

"After these things the word of the Lord came unto Abram in a vision. I am thy shield and thy exceedingly great reward".

God confirmed himself to Abram in a vision and opened up his future and the future of his seed that his generations would inherit the promise because of one man's faithfulness.

## Taking the right path

Take the right path – the righteous path with Godly conviction and pursue the God of freedom and liberty.

Psalms Chapter 37 v 23

"The steps of a good man are ordered by the Lord: and he delights in his way"

What a privilege knowing that your steps are directed by the Lord. The Lord Jesus issues guidance with divine favour that will lighten up his and her way.

A good man and a good woman will walk in revelation when their feet are spiritually prepared for purpose and destiny.

God's word has all the instructions that we need to signpost us to the right path and to sustain us on the narrow road. God removes blindness, enabling us to see the right path clearly; he releases a desire to the walk in the right path and empowers us with strength to follow the footprints of the Saviour.

## Laughter

All of our emotions were given to us by God, be they happiness, sadness or fear. All have their place. Fear for example is given to us as an indicator of danger. The person without fear is in danger for they will walk into situations and put themselves at risk without taking precautions.

God has given us laughter so we can demonstrate our enjoyment or happiness laughter is also a kind of medicine for it helps our heart.

Proverbs Chapter 15 v 13 and 15

"A merry heart makes a cheerful countenance"

"All the days of the afflicted are evil: but he that is of a merry heart hath a continual feast".

Our disposition is related to our health. If we are miserable I believe that this will lead to an unhappy life and even shorten it. However a merry heart and a positive mindset can make life more enjoyable giving us a healthier heart.

From a physiological perspective laughter releases feel good hormones and raises our mood. We are emotional beings and it is important that we are in touch with them. Christians have plenty of things to laugh about: Being placed in Christ means that we are protected from the evil one. God watches over us and he is our defence and we can run to him in times of need or distress.

The next time we face difficulty all we need to do is to use our faith and God will give us the ability to laugh at them for he has already given us the victory.

## Peace in the storm

To have peace, God has to have perfected his peace in our life, so when you are in the eye of the storm and facing pressures of life, be assured that the Peace maker is at the helm guiding you to safety.

Luke Chapter 8 v 24

"The disciples went and woke him saying Master, Master we're going down, Jesus got up and rebuked the wind and the raging waters the storm subsided and all was calm"

The book of Luke is the longest of the Gospels written in AD 60, particularly for the Greeks its emphasis is about the humanity of Christ, Jesus is presented as the Son of Man.

Two people can be going through turbulent situations. The one without peace is overwhelmed by the storm. The other person recognises that Jesus Christ is their peace and they remain untouched by the storm.

## God's plan for you

God the creator of all mankind has a purpose and destiny in mind for everyone unique to their characteristics, God created the earth with you in mind.

The book of Jeremiah was written in the 7th century BC, he was a young priest of Anathoth when he began to prophesy.

Jeremiah Chapter 29 v 11

"For I know the plans I have for you declares the Lord, plans to prosper you and not to harm you, plans to give you hope and a future" (Insight Bible)

"For I know the thoughts that I think towards you says the Lord thoughts of peace and not evil to give you an expected end" (KJV)

God gives all believers a life structure and design, his strategy is to develop you and restore his confidence in you. Release his anointing of continuing success for your future.

Lean on your Heavenly Father when you feel weak, he will give you the strength to carry on.

## Standing on a firm foundation

There are two types of foundations.

1.      Firstly, one that has a foundation that consists of brick and mortar.

2.      Secondly, the spiritual foundation that has its roots in Jesus Christ.

In Christ's Sermon on the Mount he exalts his disciples and followers in Matthew Chapter 7 v 24 – 27

Therefore everyone who hears these words of mine and puts them into practice is like a wise man who built his house on the rock.

The rain came down, the streams rose and the winds blew and beat against the house, yet it did not fall, because it had its foundation on the rock but everyone who hears these words of mine and does not put them into practice is like a foolish man who built his house on the sand.

The rain came down, the streams rose and the winds blew and beat against that house and it fell with a great crash.

Jesus told the parable to teach his disciples and followers Christian principles and the character that they would need to develop to be able to stand on a firm foundation.

**The house on the sand**

If you disobey God's command

1.    Foolishly replacing God's wisdom

2.    If you neglect your duty of service to the Lord you will be carried away by false hope, false trust and failure.

## The house on the rock is important to all

1.    Challenging believers to be obedient to Christ and his teachings.

2.    Encouraging us to be led by Godly wisdom.

3.    Enabling us to maintain a spiritual foundation through prayer and by studying daily and meditating on the word of God.

4.    God will prove himself faithful to all those who believe in him that the rain of circumstances and the strong under

current of the stream will not cause you to lose your footing.

Covet the qualities of the house on the rock; let the rain come, let the wind blow let the stream rise. Once you are rooted in God's word you can shelter in the rock which is Jesus Christ.

## Take the Limit off God

A lack of confidence will cause us to put restrictions on using our Godly potential, fear causes us to put limits on ourselves by bringing clouds of despair into our lives and the lives of others. God has never placed a limit on us he has given us a free will to make wise decisions about our future, God has invested his best in us that it would be a shame to waste it.

In the reservoir of life there is a plentiful supply of God's goodness and mercy once we acknowledge that Jesus Christ is central to our existence.

Let us draw strength from the scripture.

Ephesians 3 v 20

'Now unto him that is able to do exceedingly abundantly above all that we ask or think according to the power that works in us'

When you take the limit off God, he takes pleasure in fulfilling his promise in our life more than we could ever dream. God wants to put a positive spin on our present life circumstances and problems. Having a negative mindset towards the best Jesus Christ has for us, makes us losers not winners.

We are champions, the battle of doubt and insecurity has been beaten in Jesus name. Praising God that he has the key to every emotional, physical, Spiritual and mental limit, continual worship and thanks giving to God bring victory to the fore.

## Open Doors

John the Baptist in Matthew Chapter 11 was a forerunner for his Cousin Jesus Christ. He craved out a unique ministry path for Jesus to follow and unusual doors started to open.

Open doors are God's opportunity to show his faithfulness to you as his treasured possession. Presenting your body has a living offering to the Lord, and walking in integrity enables believers to develop a covenant relationship with the King of Kings and Lord of Lords.

If you have a gift of singing dedicate your gift and dreams onto the Lord and practise until you have perfected your gift. The Bible makes reference to this, it is called stimulating your gift, volunteer for the worship team, or join a group or choir God will cause you to find favour with a mentor to support and shape your ministry for your destiny.

When a new vision is birthed within a believer, one receives a new revelation of who Jesus Christ is. He uses individuals to proclaim the Gospel of Jesus Christ to people whose hearts are ripe to receive the good news.

## Be Blessed

The ultimate blessing experience comes through Jesus Christ. Our life is impacted by the gift of life he gives to us.

There is a two fold ministry to blessing.

Blessing the Lord; in the good and bad seasons of our life.

Through our one to one conversation with the Father, in prayer, intercession, praise and psalms, Jesus responds almost immediately and begins to bless us. On other occasions he takes time to build our character spiritually through his Holy Spirit reviving our patience by binding our faith and trust together.

And bringing us into favour with God where he releases bountiful blessing upon us more than we could dream or imagine.

Psalms Chapter 34, David changed his behaviour (pretended to be insane) before Abimelech who drove him away, and he departed.

David strength was restored and he said

*    I will bless the Lord at all times

*    In the best of times

*    In the worse of times

*    I will not curse God

*    His praise shall continually be in my mouth

*      I will not stop praising and glorifying God

*      I will participate in worship and thanks-
       giving from the rising of the Sun until
       nightfall the praises of God will be on my
       lips.

Like David I can be reminded of the steadfast
love of the Lord towards me. God is always
blessing me and I have learnt I can be a blessing
to others.

## Steadfast Faith

The New Testament Epistle of James sources faith to the believer.

Faith has its origin in Jesus Christ.

James Chapter 2 v 26

"For as the body without the Spirit is dead, so faith without works is dead also"

The body refers to the spirit of man. Faith is an action word. God wants to us adopt his attributes and qualities; this comes through having a personal relationship with Jesus Christ and with the Holy Spirit who administers his gifts through us.

Our faith has to be firm but still remain rooted in the living word of God. Faith and confidence is often stretched to the point of being shattered into pieces. Jesus steps in and rescues us after a period of thinking that you are on your own. God shows up miraculously through a friend giving a gift, or a scripture full of comfort that is illuminated through our Bible devotion and this causes our faith to bounce back.

David was a shepherd of the sheep and Jesus makes reference to himself as the good shepherd, he tends to the sheep in the pasture of life and keeps them from predators that seek to destroy their steadfast faith.

## Stand your ground do not waiver

There is always a reason why an individual feels strongly about a situation and choose to stand in the face of adversity and life challenges.

God help those who help themselves.

In the third chapter of Daniel three Hebrew Counsellors set over the affairs of the province of Babylon they were Shadrach, Meshach and Abednego stood their ground by not bowing to the image of gold that King Nebuchadnezzar had set up for the people of the kingdom to worship. This enraged the King but they did not waiver even though death stared them in the face.

1.  They took their stand with confidence.

2.  They took a stand of conviction without the fear of intimidation.

3.  Thrown into the furnace God sent his Son to support them, the God of truth will give you the courage to stand your ground without hesitation.

## The Chosen One

To be chosen means to be special, but this still does not exempt us from challenges and adversity.

In 1$^{st}$ Peter Chapter 2 v 9

"But you are a chosen people a royal priesthood, a holy nation, a people belonging to God. That you may declare the praises of him who called you out of darkness into his wonderful light"

The priesthood of the Christian is therefore a birthright, just as every descendant of Aaron was born to the priesthood. But when Christ died, the curtain a type of Christ human body was torn, so that now all believers have equal access to God, in the Holy of the Holiest.

1.  Chosen, but still waiting to be discovered

2.  Chosen for a purpose

3.  Chosen on purpose

4.  Chosen with a destiny in mind

5.  Chosen to bring glory to the kingdom has a kingdom builder

# Chapter 4

## Women of Excellence

## By Ruth Turner

The Bible gives many accounts of women of excellence who possess a God given talent to lead. Their destiny is to provide direction and purpose and to encourage women of influence to rise up and be an inspiration to other women. They are role models and mentors to others, portraying the qualities of substance that embraces the very fabric of hope, faith and charity. In the 1$^{st}$ epistle of Paul the Apostle to the Corinthians brethren, he states 'but the greatest of these is **'Charity'.**

One of the notable women featured in the Old Testament was Ruth. The author of the Book of Ruth is unknown and was written in the 10$^{th}$ Century BC. The theme of the book is Kinsman-Redeemer, and is known in the world of literature to be a masterpiece of narratives. In Ruth the events that are set forth are contemporary with the first half of the Judges where there was bloodshed and strife and lawlessness.

Orpah and Ruth had been previously married to Naomi's sons Mahlon and Chillon, after a period of time their husbands died, and both daughter in law's stayed in the family home to support Naomi, their Mother in law. During this time Naomi heard some exceptionally good news that the Lord of the harvest had visited her home the land of Moab and had prospered her people, excited at the prospect she wanted to return home. Naomi could not offer her daughter in law's solace and like any good mother in law she begged them to return to their own homeland. Orpah was easily persuaded and after an emotional farewell she left, but Ruth held tightly unto her mother in law. Relations between Moab and Israel were very volatile, during this period (Judges Chapter 3) and Ruth could not be sure of a good welcome into a country which in any case was hostile to foreigners for religious reasons.

Naomi's motherly influence and the power of the God she served greatly impacted Ruth's life she, felt compelled to follow her Mother in law, choosing to leave her family, tradition and homeland to follow her destiny.

### Ruth Chapter 1 v 16 & 17

*'And Ruth said entreat me not to leave thee or to return from following after thee, for whither thou goest I will go and where thou lodgest I will lodge thy people shall be my people, and thy God my God Where thou diest, will I die and there will I be buried, Lord do so to me and more also if ought but death part thee and me'*

Ruth had a passion for the true and living God and to support her mother in law. Naomi's attempt to dissuade Ruth made her more determined to hold unto her Mother in law. Naomi was bitter and sad from her painful life experience, but Ruth's words brought reassurance to her, 'never ask me to leave you' pleading 'please let me go with you. If you are tired on your journey I will be there to support you. If you faint by the way I will carry you. '

W. Cooper wrote the hymn:

'God moves in a mysterious ways his wonders to perform: He plans his footsteps in the sea and rides upon the storm'.

God had a prefect plan for her future. The two women travelled the long dusty roads until they eventually arrived in Bethlehem.

The town was stirred with emotion because of them, the women questioned among themselves, they recognised one of the new women back in town as Naomi. Because of

Ruth's commitment and determination in relocating to Moab and her conscious effort to provide for her family, she met Boaz and had a son called Obed her generation was blessed and became descendants to King David, the Warrior and the Psalmist.

There are numerous women that have succeeded against the odds. They gained tremendous courage strength from weakness and became women of courage.

Four steps to being a Woman of Substance

### 1. Courage

Ruth was courageous because she was prepared to leave her comfort zone, her people, her gods and follow her convictions.

## 2. Integrity

Ruth remained committed reaffirming her determination to Naomi her mother in law and her faith in God.

## 3. Supportive

Ruth negotiated employment with Boaz as a reaper to support her family.

## 4. Faithfulness

Ruth sowed the seed of kindness generously and with true perseverance reaped a bountiful harvest.

History is full of women who have reacted to events with tremendous courage and determination, the Bible records Deborah as one of the outstanding leaders in history.

In the book of Judges Deborah was willing to accept the challenge by calling upon God. After 20 years of unbearable circumstances the Israelites finally turned to God for help.

Deborah's leadership role as a judge and Advisor to the Israeli Military Army was crucial after the previous defeats against the Canaanite Army.

Deborah used her gift as a prophetess to instruct and encourage the Military General Barak to go into battle confident that God would give him victory.

Courage and character is important in leadership and Deborah possessed both qualities she was a mediator, counsellor and confidant. She gained respect because she influenced the nation of Israel to live for God after the battle.

Concluding with these points:-

*Courage*

Be a person that faithfully steps out at God's command, even if it means you do so alone.

*Leadership*

God can choose anyone to lead his people.

Young or Mature

Male or Female

Be open, be honest, don't prejudge the people God may have chosen to lead, he may have Chosen you.